A DAY IN THE LIFE OF
AN AFRICAN
ELEPHANT

Anthony Hall-Martin

SOUTHERN
BOOK PUBLISHERS

CONTENTS

TITLE PAGE: BACHELOR PARADE - ADULT BULL ELEPHANTS OFTEN FORM SOCIAL GROUPS WHICH MOVE AND FEED TOGETHER FOR A SHORT WHILE.

THESE PAGES: PLAYING FOLLOW MY LEADER, AN ELEPHANT HERD CROSSES THE CHOBE RIVER (NORTHERN BOTSWANA) ON A SANDBANK.

PAGE 1: A LARGE GROUP OF ELEPHANTS AT VOI (TSAVO EAST NATIONAL PARK, KENYA) CONJURES UP VISIONS OF AFRICAN SCENES THAT ARE NOW THE EXCEPTION RATHER THAN THE RULE.

YESTERDAY

ELEPHANTS IN AFRICA

Like man, the elephant originated and evolved in Africa. On this continent the ancestors of both species emerged, changed and died out. Each left a trace of their passing in the fossil record, and each contributed some features to their descendants; features that were eventually polished and perfected to produce the two species we know today – the African elephant *Loxodonta africana* and modern *Homo sapiens*.

The oldest clearly recognisable fossils of an ancestral elephant come from Fayum in Egypt and are about 60 million years old. Later primitive elephants, also from Fayum, had tusks in both upper and lower jaws and showed evidence of a rudimentary trunk. These features, and many others, can be linked via other primitive elephant-like forms in the fossil record to the mastodons, mammoths and living elephants of both Africa and Asia.

The ancestors of the African and Asian elephants lived together in Africa for several million years. The Asian ancestor, of the genus *Elephas*, left Africa to colonise much of Europe, the Middle East and Asia. One of the *Elephas* descendants, known as *Elephas iolensis*, was still found in East Africa as recently as 40 000 years ago. Its remains have been found at Early Stone Age sites of modern man. *Elephas iolensis* and its ancestor *E. reckii* were savanna and woodland inhabitants. The forest was occupied by *Loxodonta adaurora*, the immediate ancestor of the modern African elephant *L. africana*, which almost certainly evolved in the forest environment. Fossil remains of *L. africana* appear for the first time in deposits as young as about half a million years old. Its evolution as a forest species is still reflected in the modern forest elephant *L. africana cyclotis*, one of the two subspecies of the African elephant. The *Elephas* lineage in the savanna died out less than 40 000 years ago, leaving a vacant niche that was then occupied by the modern savanna elephant *L. a. africana*. It grew larger than the forest elephant, filling the savannas, and became the dominant mammal on the continent. So the African savanna elephant has shared its habitat with man for a mere 40 000 years.

For most of the period in which elephants and man have occupied this huge continent, there has been intense competition between the two highly adaptable and successful species. Both prefer areas of fertile soils and high rainfall – for man these are the best areas for crops and livestock, and for elephants these are the best feeding areas. Man can, of course, adapt to arid areas and live in deserts. Elephants can also do this, but wherever the two species have chosen to live they have competed with one another.

Studies in East Africa dating from the 15th century and earlier have produced clear evidence of alternating cycles of abundance and dominance between elephants and humans. At times human societies developed dense populations at the expense of elephants. At other times human numbers declined because of disease (such as sleeping sickness) and war, and elephants regained their territory. The situation was similar in West Africa, where the Mali and Ghana empires developed at the expense of elephant range.

With the advent of firearms in the 17th century, the establishment of Arab and European trading posts along the East and West African coasts, the development of the slave trade and the growing demand for ivory in the West, the equation changed dramatically. More and more elephants

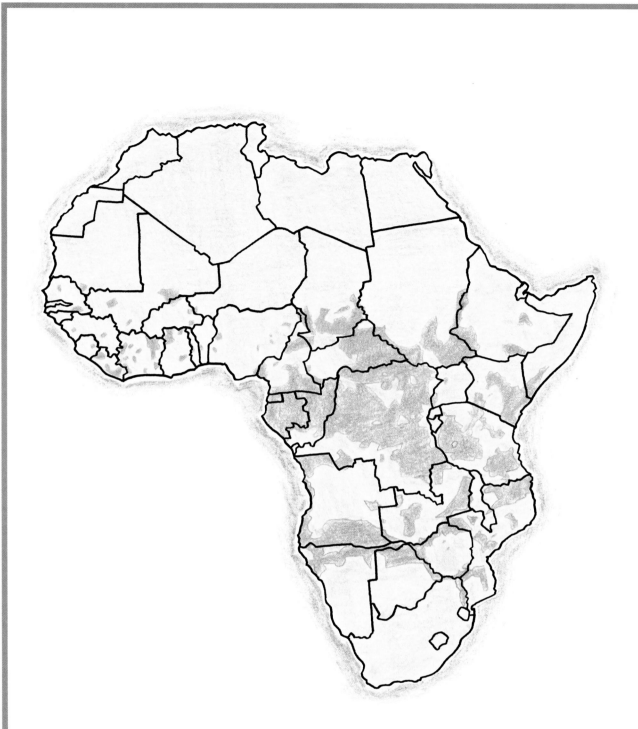

AFRICAN ELEPHANT RANGE AND PROTECTED AREAS.

were shot for their ivory in the interior, and the tusks were transported to the coast by slaves. Elephant numbers began to decline. European colonisation and settlement speeded up the process. In South Africa, where Europeans settled in 1652, the decline of elephants was most rapid. By 1790 ivory hunting was an established profession and elephants were wiped out over large areas. By 1900 there were only about 120 elephants left in the entire country. A similar pattern occurred throughout the rest of southern and sub-Saharan Africa – except for the equatorial forests where elephant numbers were not as dramatically reduced as in the savanna and woodland zones.

The colonial governments of sub-Saharan Africa, aided by the many missionary societies active on the continent, were responsible for the rapid stabilisation of political boundaries and societies from the late 19th century. Development of modern medical and health facilities, the ending of the slave trade, the introduction of many technological innovations such as railways, and settled plantation agriculture resulted in a dramatic change to Africa's social, political and economic fabric. This had two main effects on the elephants. In the first place human populations started to increase dramatically; the continental population rose from 100 million people in 1890 to 400 million by 1975, with a projected population of 814 million by the year 2000. Secondly, the colonial administrators recognised early that elephants were being eliminated almost throughout their range. The first colonial attempt at setting aside areas for the protection of wildlife, including elephants, dates from 1894 with the proclamation of the St. Lucia Game Reserve in South Africa. Subsequently most countries set aside areas as game reserves, national parks and forest reserves where elephants were legally protected, and where their numbers subsequently increased dramatically.

But these reserves were not the first or only efforts at elephant conservation. Many African societies had structured systems of land use incorporating traditional areas where animals were only hunted at certain times and under certain circumstances. The Zulu King Shaka proclaimed a royal hunting ground between the Black and White Umfolozi rivers where only he had the right to hunt. It was a very effective game reserve that was later taken over by the colonial authorities.

As people started growing cash crops in addition to traditional subsistence farming and the first timber was exploited, the conflict between man and elephants increased. This led to the creation of game departments of one kind or another in virtually all African countries. Their function was to administer wildlife reserves where they existed, but more important in most cases was the function of "crop protection" or "elephant control", during which tens of thousands of elephants were officially shot every year. In many countries large tracts of land inhabited by elephants and other wildlife were also "cleared" for settlement, or in attempts to control the spread of wildlife diseases to which cattle were vulnerable, such as trypanosomiasis. The combination of development, the ivory trade, and the growing pressure of human populations all worked against the African elephant.

By the 1960s when the colonial powers largely withdrew from Africa, leaving behind numerous independent states, only a small percentage of savanna elephants were found in game reserves, safari hunting areas and national parks. In the equatorial forests of countries such as Zaire, Gabon, Congo, Cameroon and Côte d'Ivoire, large numbers of elephants of the small forest variety were also found, mostly outside formally protected areas. During that decade the price of ivory started to rise and large-scale ivory hunting became a new threat to elephant populations, particularly in East Africa. Between 1970 and 1980 the large-scale illegal poaching of elephants for their ivory, which was exported to the Far East, gathered momentum. The ivory poaching coincided with a certain laxity of controls in most African countries following the numerous political changes of the post-independence era. Corruption involving politicians, police and customs officials in many countries aided and abetted the growing illegal ivory trade. By 1980 it was evident that elephant populations were declining catastrophically everywhere except in southern Africa.

The drop in elephant numbers was so dramatic in countries like Kenya, Uganda, Central African Republic and Zambia that Western conservationists launched a widespread, sustained campaign to ban the trade in ivory. This campaign culminated in the CITES listing of the African elephant in Appendix 1 at a 1989 meeting in Lausanne, Switzerland. CITES is the acronym for the

"Convention on International Trade in Endangered Species of Wild Fauna and Flora" – an international treaty to which most countries in the world are signatories. The Appendix 1 listing effectively banned all international trade in elephant products and the ivory trade in particular. The ban effectively closed down the major market for raw ivory in Hong Kong and the market for carved ivory in the West. The large-scale ivory trade has now ceased, but elephant poaching continues in some countries.

The negative side of the ivory trade ban, and a different perspective on the relationship between man and elephants, are to be seen in the countries of southern Africa. In Zimbabwe, Botswana, Namibia, and South Africa elephant populations, well protected within national parks, have been steadily increasing while elephant numbers elsewhere in Africa have declined. While the continental population dropped from 1,3 million in 1979 to 609 000 in 1989, the elephant population in these southern African countries increased at a rate of about 5% per annum. These growing populations, mostly confined within the boundaries of national parks and game reserves, have been responsible for increasing levels of habitat damage and change. The wildlife management authorities of these countries, particularly Zimbabwe and South Africa, have therefore followed policies of active elephant population control over the past two decades in an attempt to limit elephant destruction of the habitat. This has resulted in the culling of thousands of elephants and the utilisation of their carcasses. Elephant meat, skins and ivory are the major products of these culling operations. The revenue generated from the sale of these elephant products was seen as a positive economic contribution from the parks, and a sustained use of natural resources. In the Kruger National Park in South Africa the revenue generated from the culling of surplus elephants paid for the massive effort required to control poaching, and for other aspects of elephant management such as the census and monitoring of the populations. The CITES ban not only ended the ivory trade, which was arguably a threat to some elephant populations, but it also ended the trade in elephant skins from the culling operations in Zimbabwe and South Africa wich were carried out because of an overpopulation of elephants.

The emotional link between man and elephants is seen clearly in the overwhelming public support in the West for the ivory trade ban. Most people are unaware that the ban has done little more than allow some corrupt African governments, such as Kenya, to escape the consequences of their own inadequacies. At the same time the ban penalises the enviable management records of countries like Zimbabwe, which are now forced to accept lower elephant management and protection budgets. The elephant populations of Zimbabwe and South Africa are no longer a sustainable resource generating the means for their protection, but a burden on the fiscus of developing countries whose priorities lie with people. If, on balance, the ivory trade ban results in a secure future for the African elephant, it would be uncharitable to oppose it. The reality of Africa, however, is that the inevitable competition between elephants and man for land and living space continues. In time the only elephants left in Africa will be those that can be accommodated within national parks and game reserves. The rest will be sacrificed to agriculture. At the most Africa's protected areas, including many yet to be established, will be able to accommodate no more than 250 000–300 000 elephants. It is painfully obvious that the rest will be killed. The ivory trade ban served no purpose other than to express the moral outrage of modern Western man. Its role in conserving elephants is meaningless. This species will only survive if the interest in elephants can be sustained and used to generate the money, training, legislation, infrastructure and effort required to create and manage national parks where the elephant and other wildlife and natural ecosystems can survive.

PAGES 6 & 7: THE KRUGER NATIONAL PARK IN SOUTH AFRICA BOASTS SOME OF THE GREATEST TUSKERS OF RECENT YEARS, INCLUDING JOAO (ABOVE), SHAWU (LEFT) WHOSE LEFT TUSK IS ONE OF THE LONGEST ON RECORD AT 319 CM, AND MANDLEVE (RIGHT), NOW IN HIS TWILIGHT YEARS.

PAGES 8 & 9: ELEPHANTS IN THE ADDO ELEPHANT NATIONAL PARK (SOUTH AFRICA) STROLLING ON A CARPET OF FLOWERS.

DAWN

WHERE THEY ROAM

The African elephant, like man and the leopard, is found in every habitat type that this diverse continent has to offer. While elephant numbers have halved over the past decade alone, and their effective range has continued to shrink, in 1989 there were still an estimated 609 000 elephants occupying a range of 5,8 million square kilometres. In the middle of the 18th century, however, elephants were found in their millions and their range was probably about 16,5 million square kilometres.

Elephants tolerate a wide range of climatic conditions from the hot, humid tropical climates of the rainforest zone of West and Equatorial Africa at one extreme to the cool, dry desert of Namibia on the other. Nighttime temperatures in Namibia can drop to several degrees below freezing. In other areas where elephants are found, or were once found, they regularly coped with freezing overnight temperatures. Over most of their range, however, the climate is generally hot in summer and mild during the winter months.

The most important determinants of habitat quality for elephants are the presence of a wide variety of good quality food, adequate trees to provide shade during the heat of the day, permanent water in the form of perennial rivers or springs that hold water through the dry season, salt licks and mud wallows. In many areas the habitat may be adequate in one season only, as in places where there is only enough water in temporary rainwater pools during the rainy season. When these pools dry up at the onset of winter, the elephants have to move to other areas. Elephants usually drink every day, but in exceptionally arid areas they may go for as long as several days at a time without drinking.

In general elephants seek areas with good soils and high rainfall. In such areas their population densities are highest – provided man is absent. In less attractive environments elephants may well survive adequately but at much lower densities than in prime habitat.

After Asia, the continent of Africa is the second largest on earth, covering an area of about 30 million square kilometres. Some of the oldest rocks in the world, dating back to the beginning of the planet some 4 500 million years ago, are found in Africa. Geological processes stretching over aeons of time have shaped the landscape and geomorphology. Mountains have risen and been eroded away. Volcanoes have erupted and covered the land in lava, which in turn has eroded over time and the material deposited elsewhere as soil or mud. The interaction of geological events and climate has produced different rocks, soils, landscapes and environments in which plants have formed different vegetation types or plant communities. All these processes have combined to form the diversity of habitats where elephants roam.

Much of Africa, and virtually the whole of West Africa, is flat and fairly featureless with very little topographical diversity. A few isolated plateau areas such as the Fouta Djallon in Guinea and the Jos Plateau of Nigeria break the monotony. In the Sahara to the north the Tibesti, Air and Hoggar massifs rise out of flat country. The eastern half of the continent is much more mountainous,

rising to massive peaks like Mt Kenya, Kilimanjaro in Tanzania and Mulanje in Malawi. Extensive mountain ranges are a feature of the southern part of the continent and the Ethiopian highlands in the north. A dominant feature of the east is the Great Rift Valley system that stretches from Ethiopia to Malawi.

The equatorial regions of Africa (from about 10°N to 15°S of the equator) experience higher and more reliable rainfall than the rest of the continent. As one moves away from the equator the rainfall steadily declines. The dry season lasts longer the further north or south one goes until eventually the semi-desert climate of the Sahel in the north and the Kalahari in the south is reached. In these regions elephants can only survive where perennial rivers rising in higher rainfall areas bring water to the semi-desert – such as the Niger River in the Sahel and the Okavango River in Botswana.

The zones or bands of decreasing rainfall are fairly closely reflected in the composition of the vegetation of Africa. Thus the high-rainfall equatorial regions support evergreen forest or rainforest. Further away from the equator the vegetation changes to woodland, where trees are spaced further from one another and a luxuriant growth of tall grasses replaces the shrub undergrowth of the forest. As rainfall decreases further the woodland gives way to savanna, where the grass is less abundant and most trees drop their leaves during the dry season. The savanna gives way to shrubs and sparse grasses in the Sahel of the north and the Kalahari and Karoo of the south; then to the Sahara with little vegetation at all. On the south-west coast lies the Namib, also a sand desert with little vegetation. These broad bands of vegetation are interrupted by mountains in the east, which introduce great complexity. They are also intersected by rivers. Most rivers support a more abundant riverine thicket or gallery forest and so effectively extend the vegetation typical of higher rainfall areas into the arid zones. The Great Rift Valley on the eastern side of the continent, which is characterised by volcanic mountains and lakes, also complicates this rough description of the vegetation zones of Africa. The Mediterranean coast north of the Atlas Mountains, and the southern tip of the continent at the Cape of Good Hope, have a totally different climatic system characterised by winter rainfall, dry summers and a sclerophyllous type of vegetation.

The great adaptability of elephants and the fact that they can vary their diet according to circumstances – eating mainly grass in some areas or at some times of the year, and concentrating on browsing at other times – allows them great flexibility of habitat selection. They are therefore found from areas as diverse as swamps and rainforest to arid sun-baked deserts. They occupy virtually all varieties of woodland, savanna and thickets and in some areas extensive grassland plains; rocky hills, rugged mountains and semi-desert scrub are all equally acceptable.

Elephants are still found in 36 African countries, and have also recently been re-introduced to Swaziland where they were last seen in the wild in 1870. By 1989 at least 10 countries had fewer than 1 000 elephants, another 11 countries had fewer than 5 000 elephants each and only 5 countries had populations greater than 50 000 elephants. The mean number of elephants per African country was only 16 916. However, a more important statistic is the mean size of each discrete population of elephants. In West Africa, for example, this figure is below 20 which means that the long-term chances of survival of many, if not most, elephant populations are small. The only large populations still extant, with a reasonable hope of long-term survival, are those no longer in competition with man – effectively those in Africa's national parks. Clearly the only African elephants that will survive into the 21st century will be those in the national parks. That is why the adequate funding, protection and management of these areas are so vital for the African elephant.

PAGES 14 & 15: MARCHING PLACIDLY ACROSS A DEAD LAKE, THE AMBOSELI ELEPHANTS MOVE TOWARDS THE LUSH LORIAN SWAMP AT THE FOOT OF MOUNT KILIMANJARO IN SEARCH OF FOOD AND WATER.

PAGE 17: ELEPHANTS OF THE MIOMBO WOODLANDS, CENTRAL AFRICA, HAVE NARROW HEADS AND SMALL TUSKS.

THIS PAGE: A STOCKY, SHORT-TUSKED ELEPHANT OF NAMIBIA'S DESERT AREAS. THESE ELEPHANTS' BRITTLE TUSKS ARE EASILY BROKEN GIVING THEM THEIR CHARACTERISTIC APPEARANCE.

LEFT: AERIAL SHOT OF ELEPHANTS AND EGRETS ROAMING ON THE FLOODPLAINS OF LIWONDE, MALAWI.

TOP: A SMALL HERD OF DESERT ELEPHANTS IN THE KAOKOVELD, NAMIBIA. THEY ARE PERFECTLY ADAPTED TO LIFE IN THE DESERT THROUGH FASTIDIOUS FEEDING HABITS AND THE ABILITY TO GO WITHOUT WATER FOR DAYS ON END.

ABOVE: DESERT ELEPHANTS IN DAMARALAND, NAMIBIA, WANDER THROUGH A BARREN LANDSCAPE WHERE MOST OF THE PLANTS ARE DROUGHT-ADAPTED SUCCULENTS.

ABOVE: TWO CATTLE EGRETS HITCH A RIDE ACROSS THE ZAMBEZI RIVER.

RIGHT: THE FLOODPLAINS AND SWAMPS OF THE SHIRE RIVER (LIWONDE NATIONAL PARK, MALAWI) OFFER AN ABUNDANCE OF GREEN GRASS DURING THE DRY SEASON WHEN THERE IS LITTLE FOOD LEFT IN THE WOODLANDS.

BELOW: THE ELEPHANTS OF FOSSE-AUX-LIONS (NORTHERN TOGO) SHOW CHARACTERISTICS OF BOTH FOREST AND SAVANNA ELEPHANTS. THIS IS COMMON IN THE TRANSITION ZONE BETWEEN FOREST AND WOODLAND IN WEST AND EQUATORIAL AFRICA.

OVERLEAF: A BABY ELEPHANT SAFE AND SECURE UNDER THE BELLY OF HER MOTHER.

MORNING

BIRTH AND GROWING UP

Elephant calves, born after a gestation period of about 22 months, enter a complex social environment in which they are the centre of attention. For elephant babies the world is dominated not only by a caring mother but by aunts, siblings and numerous relatives who all play a role in raising, protecting and caring for the young. Elephant society is divided by sex into two separate and different systems, with totally different objectives and demands. Males live in solitude or the company of other males from the age of puberty onwards. For elephant females the social organisation is geared to the successful raising of calves.

The basic unit of elephant society is the mother and her female calves. Females are born into the family group and remain with it throughout their lives – which can be 55–60 years. The family group is led by a senior cow, known as the matriarch, whose female offspring and relatives make up the rest of the group. Males only stay with the family until puberty, when they leave for the life of bachelor bulls in male home ranges. These elephant families can have as few as 2–6 members if a young cow is setting up a group on her own or with a sister, or as many as 20–30 animals in a well-established group. The death of a matriarch is often the stimulus for the splitting up of a large family herd. The newly formed herds keep in touch with one another, as well as other herds in the next tier of elephant society, the kinship groups. These are linked into clans which are more distantly related, but occupy the same range or "territory". Several clans make up a distinct sub-population together with the bull ranges and their inhabitants. Each stratum of elephant society involves more animals, and therefore less intense contact and relationships.

The newborn elephant calf weighs about 120 kg and stands about 85 cm high at the shoulder. It is covered in a fairly dense coat of silky black hair, which it soon loses. The ears of the baby are spread flat on the top of the head. As it grows older the ears stand out further from the head and later they develop the typical "turn-over" of the adult. The birth of an elephant calf in the wild has only rarely been witnessed. The cow remains on her feet and is surrounded by several other cows who comfort the labouring mother and help clean the newborn calf. This assistance is the basis of the elephant "midwives" legend – the other cows also help to get the new arrival onto its feet. The birth is greeted by much commotion with elephants vocalising, rubbing against one another, and generally showing great agitation. Most animals try to touch the new calf with their trunks, to smell it and no doubt to reassure it. The new mother is very tolerant of the attention bestowed on her baby. This is, after all, the beginning of a behavioural pattern that will last for many years.

From about the age of two the females in the family assume the role of mothering the calf, referred to by scientists as "allomothering", and in shorthand as "auntying" or "nannying". The female calves play with them, care for them, help them if they get stuck in waterholes or in mud, help them negotiate obstacles like logs or rocky terrain, and guide them back to the herd or their mothers if they wander. An elephant baby is seldom more than a metre or two from another elephant and is

constantly being touched by a caring trunk. Within the family as a whole animals are usually no further than 20 metres at the most from another elephant. It is a caring, complex and stable environment for the young elephant calf. This behaviour not only ensures a secure calfhood for the baby, but it also allows the older female calves to learn and practise the skills and responsibilities of motherhood that they themselves will require a little later.

The calf has to practise the use and manipulation of its trunk, a complex business that is seldom mastered before the age of three months. Before then it swings the trunk around more like a sloppy garden hose than the precise organ of balance, control and sensitivity that it eventually becomes. Elephant calves suckle from their mothers for at least two years, sometimes a little longer. They do not drink with their trunks, as the unobservant might suppose. They take the nipple into their mouths to suck like other mammals, with the trunk folded up out of the way. By about six months of age elephant calves are also taking leaves, grass and other plant food with their trunks – not always efficiently, but with gradually increasing skill. Elephants learn what to eat from watching their mothers and "aunties".

Quite often they take plant material out of the mouth of an older animal, so learning what is palatable and edible.

Much of the elephant calf's day is occupied in play. They run around together, butting and pushing each other, climbing over one another and over older animals that happen to be lying down. They frolic in mudholes with older calves and if they slip, fall or get stuck, there is always a nanny nearby to help. If the calf gets into real trouble the mother is never far away. Even at an early age there is a divergence in play patterns between males and females. Male calves spend more time in aggressive head butting and pushing play, and later in play fighting. When an elephant calf mounts another in play, as they often do, the chances are that it is a male calf. Females spend more time in "mothering" play, learning the skills that they will need in the future.

As calves grow up they spend less time in the boisterous play of the very young, and more time in serious activities. Females six years and older are the leaders in allomothering and make the most devoted nannies. Young males of the same age spend more time learning to fight and establishing their position in the hierarchy among the other males of their own age. Females generally attain functional sexual maturity at an earlier age than males. Females may come into oestrous as early as eight or nine years of age and can then be mated. The first mating is an unsettling experience for a young cow, largely because of the great difference in size between herself (at about 1 200 kg) and the bull who will mate her (as heavy as 5 000 kg). Nevertheless the females are able to support the great weight of the bulls, who rest their forefeet on the back of the cow when mating. The mating, like every other facet of elephant life, occurs in the presence of the family group. The anxiety of the virgin cow is allayed by the presence of the older cows and siblings who gather round and support her during the mating.

Young bulls 12–14 years of age are sexually mature though not yet behaviourally mature. Cows do not allow such youngsters to mate with them. At this age however the young bulls spend more and more time away from the herd or with other young bulls of the same age. At this time they are less tolerated by the adult cows of the herd, who may be quite aggressive towards them. They gradually break their ties with their maternal group and move off to the bull areas to live bachelor lives, never again to enjoy the security of the herd.

PAGES 26 & 27: WITH THE ADULTS STANDING GUARD, THE YOUNGSTERS FROLIC IN A MUD WALLOW.

PAGES 28 & 29: TOLERANCE, CARE AND PLAYFULNESS MARK THE RELATIONSHIP BETWEEN OLDER FEMALE CALVES AND THEIR YOUNG SIBLINGS.

PAGES 30 & 31: A MOTHER GENTLY HELPS HER WAKING CALF TO ITS FEET (TOP LEFT). A CALF ROMPS WITH ITS OLDER SISTER WHILE A PROUD MOTHER LOOKS ON (MIDDLE AND BOTTOM LEFT AND MAIN PICTURE).

THIS PAGE, TOP: A BABY ELEPHANT CONCENTRATES HARD ON CURLING UP ITS TRUNK.

ABOVE: WHEN SUCKLING, A YOUNG ELEPHANT TAKES THE NIPPLE IN ITS MOUTH AND KEEPS ITS TRUNK CURLED UP.

RIGHT: TWINS ARE EXTREMELY RARE AMONG ELEPHANTS, BUT CALVES OF THE SAME AGE OFTEN PLAY TOGETHER AND MAY BE LOOKED AFTER BY EITHER MOTHER.

BELOW: A BABY ELEPHANT PRACTISING AN ALARM SQUEAL WITH
EARS SPREAD WIDE AND TRUNK REACHING FORWARD.

RIGHT: ELEPHANTS GATHER AROUND A PAN IN CHOBE NATIONAL
PARK, BOTSWANA. DURING THE DRY SEASON WATERHOLES SERVE
AS A MEETING PLACE FOR ANIMALS.

PAGES 38 & 39: A HERD OF ELEPHANTS IN THE ADDO ELEPHANT
NATIONAL PARK, SOUTH AFRICA, FORM A SOLID, PROTECTIVE WALL
AROUND A YOUNG CALF AS THEY EMERGE INTO A CLEARING.

SOCIAL BEHAVIOUR AND COMMUNICATION

Like humans, elephants have a long childhood, and like human children they spend much of their youth in learning. Because they are such long-lived animals, with a lifespan of up to 60 years, elephants have time to accumulate experience and wisdom, and then to pass it on to the next generation. The length and social complexity of their lives allow elephants the luxury of several years of learning time, as compared with the months or even weeks of lesser mammals.

Elephants are highly intelligent, as well as enormously powerful and dangerous. They would thus be able to inflict severe damage upon one another if their behaviour were not regulated by social constraints and social routine. To this end they have a highly developed system of communication that utilises body movements and posture, chemical signals and complex vocalisations. The body movements are essentially an optical form of communication as the animal being addressed must be looking at the animal doing the communicating. These signals include the aggressive "standing tall" signal. In this behaviour pattern the elephant abruptly raises its head and fans its ears out so that they extend at right angles to the body to give an impression of greater size. This behaviour is essentially aimed at intimidating an opponent, particularly if the opponent is man or another animal. The elephant can exaggerate the pattern by making a short rush towards its opponent and slapping its ears hard against the head the moment before it spreads them out. This makes a loud, sharp noise, usually raises a cloud of dust and makes the action altogether far more impressive.

Among many other forms of physical social communication is the posture adopted by a cow in the presence of a dominant bull. She turns her hindquarters towards the bull, spreading her legs so that his trunk has easy access to her vulva, which he usually inspects to detect oestrous by the chemical signals in the cow's urine. She may also oblige the bull performing the oestrous test by urinating. All the while her head is held low with the ears pressed against it; the very opposite of the "standing tall" position. The bull can tell if the cow is close to oestrus by sniffing at the urine with his trunk and then transferring the scent or chemical signals to a highly sensitive organ situated in the roof of the mouth, known as a vomeronasal organ or Jacobson's organ. Other chemical signals are also interpreted in the same way with the trunk sniffing at the source of the signal and then reaching into the mouth to blow the molecules of the scent over the sensory opening of the vomeronasal organ. Elephants gain a great deal of information about their environment from chemical clues, and can also probably identify individual companions or members of other groups by their scent. This must to some extent compensate for their poor eyesight, as they cannot distinguish detail beyond 50 metres.

Elephant vocalisations are another complex form of communication. There are calls uttered by calves when they want to suckle, and answering rumbles by their mother. Squeals of delight made

by calves playing in mud or water or clambering over one another are very clear in their intent. Likewise the scream of an elephant calf that is in difficulty or has been frightened, is also readily interpreted. Other elephants respond immediately by rushing up to assist the distressed animal. Other vocalisations that may be heard include the roars of anger emitted by fighting bulls, or cows attacking young bulls to drive them away from the group. The elephant's "trumpet" or scream is particularly well known. Like other sounds it arises from the larynx but is probably modulated and resonated in the trunk. It is usually used in anger, but can also indicate excitement, as when a herd is rushing towards a waterhole.

Another major form of communication between elephants was long suspected from field observations, but only recently identified and explained by scientists. Hunters and game rangers were intrigued by the apparent ability of herds of elephants to leave an area quickly when one was shot or disturbed some distance away. It had also been noted that large formations of elephants could move in an apparently coordinated fashion over long distances, without being close enough to see one another or to hear the normal vocalisations that people could hear. This phenomenon was explained only recently when scientists discovered that elephants can also communicate by making calls at very low wavelengths, or infrasound. These sounds cannot be detected by the human ear, but a substantial body of evidence now indicates that they are heard over very long distances by other elephants. The infrasound calls made by a bull in musth may be among the most biologically useful forms of communication. These calls serve the purpose of warning other bulls of his presence, and thereby allow them to avoid contact with the musth bull. These calls can be also heard by cows, in particular by an oestrous cow who also makes an infrasound call advertising her status. This form of communication may, therefore, be a means of increasing the chances of a musth bull meeting with an oestrous cow and result in a successful mating.

For centuries it has been known that Asian elephant bulls regularly experience a condition known as "musth". During this time the temporal glands (located between the eye and the ear) are swollen and they secrete a viscous fluid that appears as a dark tear stain on the side of the elephant's face. The condition is also accompanied by a constant dribbling from the penis, which stains the bull's legs. At such times the bulls are highly aggressive towards their mahouts (handlers) and other elephants and are usually kept chained up. This condition was only recognised in African elephants during the late 1970s, but is now well documented. The blood testosterone values of musth bulls are greatly elevated above normal levels, and this explains their aggression. The behaviour associated with musth in the African elephant bull includes aggression, travelling long distances seeking contact with cows, emitting the musth call, and challenging and attacking other bulls. The testosterone boost overrides the bull's normal acceptance of a hierarchical position and spurs him to challenge bulls he would normally avoid, giving him access to cows that would normally be attended by a higher ranking bull. The musth condition in bulls is recognised by cows and they are far more compliant with musth bulls who therefore dominate matings. It is certain, therefore, that musth is linked to mating and that a musth bull has a decided advantage in fighting for position during the relatively short period when cows are in oestrus, and in gaining acceptance by cows. On the negative side of the score card is the fact that musth bulls are more likely to kill or be killed because they are more likely to engage in serious fights where ritual proceedings are abandoned in favour of murderous aggression. If, however, they have succeeded in mating at least once and passing on their genes, their death has little evolutionary importance.

PAGES 40 & 41: WHENEVER A YOUNG ELEPHANT MOVES, AN OLDER SISTER OR HERD MEMBER IS QUICK TO GUIDE AND GUARD IT, THEREBY PROVIDING THE CONSTANT COMPANIONSHIP THAT CHARACTERISES ELEPHANT SOCIAL LIFE.

THESE PAGES: APART FROM FEEDING, DRINKING AND BREATHING AN ELEPHANT'S TRUNK IS ALSO USED FOR GENTLE PHYSICAL CONTACT (TOP LEFT); THE PRELIMINARY GRAPPLING AROUND THE HEAD WHICH PRECEDES A FIGHT OR WRESTLING MATCH BETWEEN YOUNG BULLS (MIDDLE LEFT); SCENTING OF OTHER ELEPHANTS AND THEIR FOOD BY SMELLING AT THE VOMERONASAL ORGAN SITUATED IN THE PALATE (BOTTOM LEFT); AND TO SIGNIFY SUBMISSION TOWARDS A LARGER ANIMAL (RIGHT).

THESE PAGES: MOUNTING ANOTHER ELEPHANT DURING PLAY IS OFTEN STIMULATED BY A LARGER ANIMAL LYING DOWN (MAIN PICTURE). THE "STANDING TALL" POSITION WITH HEAD HELD HIGH AND EARS SPREAD WIDE IS ADOPTED TO INTIMIDATE OTHER ANIMALS (TOP LEFT). WHILE CIRCLING A HERD, A MUSTH BULL WITH TYPICAL TEAR STAINS ON HIS CHEEKS AND URINE STAINS ON HIS HIND LEGS SIGNALS HIS STATUS TO OESTROUS COWS BY CALLING INFRASONICALLY (TOP RIGHT). THE CARESSING OF A COW BY LAYING HIS TRUNK ALONG HER BACK IS USUALLY A FINAL STEP IN MATING BY WHICH THE BULL SIGNALS HIS INTENTIONS. THE COW SIGNALS HER ACCEPTANCE BY STANDING STILL (ABOVE).

PAGES 46 & 47: CONTRARY TO THEIR NORMAL BEHAVIOUR ELEPHANT HERDS CAN STAY WELL APART IF THERE IS TENSION BETWEEN THE MATRIARCHS.

PAGES 48 & 49: ELEPHANTS PREFER TO DRINK IN THE HEAT OF THE DAY. THEIR MOVING TO THE WATERHOLE AND THE DRINKING SESSION IS A HIGHLY SOCIAL EVENT.

PAGES 52 & 53: WHEN DISTURBED, THE AUTOMATIC REACTION OF A HERD IS TO CLUSTER TOGETHER, AND THEN TO ALLOW THE YOUNG TO MOVE TO THE MIDDLE WHILE THE LARGER ANIMALS FORM A PROTECTIVE WALL ON THE OUTSIDE.

MIDDAY

THE SOCIAL SYSTEM

Elephants are highly social animals. The herd, led by the matriarch, undertakes all its daily activities as a group. Whether moving, feeding, bathing, drinking or resting the herd maintains its cohesion and social order. Only old bulls and bulls in musth spend much time alone. Even then, old bulls usually have regular contact with other, younger, males that keep them company. The links between old bulls and the youngsters who are often found with them are not permanent, however, as the young bulls come and go. African hunters' explanations of the social system of elephants are astute, the young bulls keeping company with older animals are known as "askaris", which is the Swahili word for a soldier or guard. These young bulls are usually more alert and likely to detect danger, such as a hunter stalking the old bulls with heavier tusks. They usually raise the alarm or attack first, hence their name.

Elephants are not territorial in the same sense as other animals in that they have exclusive use of a particular area. Nevertheless they do have distinct home ranges occupied not only by the herd but by the larger social grouping known as the clan. In the Kruger National Park the clan can range from about 80 to between 300 and 400 animals. Radio-tracking studies have shown that the various component herds of the clan undertake coordinated movements through the home range. Contact is not maintained by sight or smell, but by infrasound communication, which elephants can hear over distances of 4 km or more.

Bulls occupy bachelor ranges that are fairly discrete and often do not overlap with the home ranges of the families. Bulls who stay within the boundaries of the home range, such as the old giants and their young askaris, may go for months without having contact with breeding herds. Bulls do wander, however, and particularly when in musth they travel great distances through breeding herd ranges looking for cows in oestrus. The musth bulls of the Kruger National Park in South Africa have been known to travel 30 km a day. At the end of the musth period they usually return to their own ranges. Within any bull range all the bulls know one another, and recognise their position within the social hierarchy. Most of the bulls within a bull range will have been recruited from neighbouring clan ranges and the chances are that they will have met one another on many occasions as they grew up. Because the bulls respect the dominance hierarchy built up over the years of play-fighting, and later on more serious fighting, they know one another's strength. Fighting between bulls that know each another is seldom fatal – except in confined areas like Addo in South Africa where animals cannot get away from a persistent attacker. In large, open systems the most likely cause of mortality is fighting between strange bulls who do not know the local hierarchy. The stranger, particularly the one in musth, then stands a greater chance of killing or being killed. The musth bull, with elevated blood testosterone levels, has an advantage equivalent to that of an athlete on steroids. He pursues his attack beyond ritual – and goes for the real thing.

In evolutionary terms the advantage enjoyed by a strange bull in musth over local bulls who are not in musth is a mechanism for outbreeding which ensures genetic diversity. The local bulls are more likely to have been born in the nearest clans, and may therefore be more closely related to the

cows. Strange musth bulls that have wandered long distances from totally unrelated clans bring genetic diversity to the population. This may also partly explain why cows prefer to mate with musth bulls, even though they do not know them, than to mate with the bulls they know.

The social life of elephants, and the particular emphasis placed on the care and protection of calves, is essential in socio-biological terms due to several characteristics of elephant biology. In the first place an elephant calf represents a valuable investment in biological terms because it is not easily replaced. A mature elephant cow is in oestrus for 2–4 days at a time, and is usually found by a musth bull and mated successfully in that time. If she misses, she repeats the cycle three weeks later, but bulls are not a permanent part of the herd so a bull must detect her condition (through chemical and sound communication) and locate her for mating. Gestation lasts 22 months – a great investment of time in a baby. The calving interval can be as short as three years, but it is more likely to be four years. If a calf is lost when young, therefore, the enormous amount of energy invested in it is also lost, and not easily replaced. Hence there is an unusual effort on the part of all herd members, not only the mother, to protect and look after calves. In the case of lions, by contrast, the gestation period is 3,5 months, the litter consists of about three cubs on average and if they die the lioness comes into oestrus within three weeks. The investment per cub is thus minimal by comparison with the investment required in elephants.

Elephants keep to a fairly regular daily routine. This is particularly true during the dry season when it is necessary to visit a particular waterhole every day, and then move off to feeding grounds that may be far from the water. Where they have not been disturbed by poaching elephants tend to drink during the heat of the day. Drinking is accompanied by showering, wallowing and even bathing if there is enough water. After drinking and cooling off the herd may spend the rest of the hot period in any nearby shade. When the afternoon heat begins to subside the elephants will move off slowly, casually feeding as they move. By evening they are feeding more intently, and this continues into the night. In the middle of the night elephants will rest, and the youngsters in particular may lie down and sleep for short periods. The herd is usually clustered together at night, whether the animals are moving, resting or feeding. During the early hours of the morning the elephant start feeding again and carry on until they return to the water to drink.

When they have been disturbed or heavily hunted, elephants will soon learn to spend most of the daytime hours hiding or feeding in the densest vegetation they can find. In this case they will not emerge into open country until after dark, and they will also drink at night.

In areas where the changes in season are dramatic, as in the savanna regions where waterholes dry up and fire can destroy all the grass in an area, elephants move to survive. These seasonal movements are akin to migrations in that they are regular movements repeated annually. The herds move to permanent water sources in their dry season concentration areas where they congregate within daily reach of water.

Once the rains have fallen and renewed the seasonal waterholes the elephants disperse again to their summer feeding grounds. These movements are usually undertaken along regular routes, and elephant paths winding through the bush are just one indicator of the permanence of their use. The roads through many mountain passes have been built on traditional elephant tracks. The ability to use such permanent trails year after year is partly due to the longevity of the elephant. There is plenty of time to learn the route and to pass on the knowledge to the next generation. The social cohesion of the group ensures that no members are left behind during the move.

PAGES 54 & 55: ELEPHANTS LOVE SUCKING UP WATER IN
THEIR TRUNKS AND THEN SPRAYING IT OVER THEIR FLANKS
AND HEADS TO COOL DOWN.

THESE PAGES: FUN AT A SMALL MUDHOLE IN THE ADDO
NATIONAL ELEPHANT PARK: A BULL STRETCHING HIS HIND
LEGS (LEFT); RUBBING HIS KNEES AND SHINS IN THE MUD
(TOP); TAKING A MUD SHOWER (ABOVE); AND RUBBING HIS
BUTTOCKS IN THE COOLING MUD (BELOW).

ELEPHANTS TAKE ON THE COLOUR OF THE SOIL OF THEIR ENVIRONMENT. ABOVE: A BULL THAT HAS WALLOWED IN THE BLACK MUD OF THE LEBOMBO PLAINS, KRUGER NATIONAL PARK. RIGHT: A BULL THAT HAS SHOWERED IN A WHITE CALCRETE WALLOW AT ADDO.

RIGHT: A dusty desert elephant bull of Namibia finds an oasis of green grass around a desert fountain in the bed of the Uniab River.

Pages 64 & 65: Two bulls drawn to water at a small rainwater pan at Savuti in the Chobe National Park, Botswana, are carefully avoiding contact by spacing themselves well away from one another.

Page 66: A tuskless cow at Amboseli, Kenya, feeding on grass. While one batch is being chewed, the next bundle that has been plucked is being carried upwards to be placed in her mouth.

Page 67: The strong spines and thorns of *Acacia* trees do not protect them against elephants although many lesser browsers would never consider tackling them.

FOOD, FEEDING, WATER

The most important daily activities of any animals are feeding and drinking. For some animals, like lions and other carnivores, this occupies only a small part of each day. Carnivores spend at least 75% of their time resting and all their other activities, including feeding, are packed into the remaining 25%. For the elephant the proportions are reversed, and they spend most of their time feeding. Those elephants in poor quality habitats, however, are forced to spend more time searching for and gathering food than animals living in productive and resource-abundant environments such as the forest edge or high-rainfall woodlands.

The secret of the elephant's successful occupation of such a wide variety of habitats across the continent lies in its catholic diet. In any area where elephants occur it is a safe assumption that they utilise more than 90% of the local plants. They eat grass, herbs, sedges and aquatic plants; bulbs, tubers, roots, fruits and flowers; bark, wood, pods and seeds; leaves and entire branches. Their food is picked or plucked from trees or shrubs, pulled down from trees up to 6 m above the ground, pulled out of the ground roots and all; picked up off the ground or dug up from under the earth. Food gathering by elephants may include breaking down, pushing over or uprooting trees, picking aquatic plants from under the water; shaking trees to dislodge fruits or pods; opening up or tearing apart thickets and shrubs.

The trunk plays a major role in all the elephant's food gathering techniques. It is sensitive and discerning with the finesse to pick a single leaf or flower, or it can strip an entire branch of leaves and branchlets with one powerful sweep. The trunk can coil around a tuft of grass, gently gain purchase and then pull the entire plant out of the ground. Or they can just as easily, and efficiently, pluck the grass stems at ground level by using their toenails as a knife to cut through the grass. Sometimes when the elephants are feeding on low-growing grasses such as those on "grazing lawns" the feet are used all the time to scrape the grass off at ground level. The grass is then gathered in heaps that are carefully shaken to remove soil and dust before being lifted to the mouth. When grasses are pulled out of the ground, roots and all, elephants employ one of several techniques to dislodge the soil and grit before eating the grass. Sometimes the entire plant is grasped by the trunk and swung through the air, then beaten against the elephant's leg several times, each blow releasing a cloud of dust and soil particles. The plants can also be swung upwards and beaten against a tusk, beaten against the ground, or even cleaned in a "grass notch" near the tip of a tusk. This notch is a groove worn across the tusk near the tip by the regular practice of pulling the grass across the tusk with the tip of the trunk while the base of the trunk is used to press the grass against the tusk. In this way the grass

is pressed hard against the ivory and the soil is rubbed off. The friction of the grass against the tusk eventually wears a distinct groove into the ivory, hence the "grass notch".

Elephants use the trunk to strip leaves off branches, gather the heap of leaves in the curled tip of the trunk, and place them in the mouth. The trunk can also be used to manoeuvre thorny branches or fruits carefully into position between the large grinding cheek teeth or molars, so that the tongue and lips are protected from the thorns. This delicate operation is carried out as a matter of course and the elephant appears to pay very little attention to it, until the final step when the teeth clamp down carefully onto the thorns. The finger-like protrusions at the tip of the trunk are dextrous and sensitive, and with these the elephant can pick up marula fruits – yellow and tasty, about the size of a small plum – one at a time and pop them into his mouth. The trunk can be used just as effectively to scoop up a heap of fruits from the ground and put them into its mouth. The tip of the trunk is used for grasping fruit, and the trunk can also serve as a suction pump. Larger, rounded fruits can be held on the tip of the trunk by suction and then flicked up into the mouth.

Tusks are regularly employed in the food gathering activities of elephants. They are used to help clean soil from food, and also as levers over which a branch can be held with a trunk so that an upward jerk of the head is usually sufficient to tear the branch off. Tusks are also used as levers for digging roots out of the soil, as well as for digging up other underground plant parts like bulbs and tubers. Elephants are usually wasteful feeders as far as human perceptions of waste and utility are concerned. They often break branches or push over entire trees and then only eat a few leaves – discarding or leaving the rest. They do not chew their food very finely, and as they are not ruminants they do not chew the cud, so the food material often passes through the elephant's digestive tract little changed from when it was swallowed. The passage time of food through the alimentary canal of an elephant is as little as 19 hours. There is, therefore, little time for digestion to occur. To keep this inefficient digestive system functioning the elephant has to maintain a constant supply of food. In fact they require about 150–200 kg fresh weight of food and 100 litres of water per day.

Elephants are fastidious about water, and whenever possible they select the cleanest available water for drinking. Quite often of course they have little choice, especially in the drier areas of Africa and during droughts. If they can, they prefer to drink running rather than standing water. Drinking is a social event and the herd members usually drink together, packed shoulder to shoulder, and then move away as a group. The trunk is as important for drinking as for feeding, as water is drawn up into the trunk, several litres at a time, then the trunk is raised and the tip inserted into the mouth. The water is then allowed to run out of the trunk into the mouth, or expelled forcefully and squirted out. The water suction system is very complex and the exact mechanism by which it works is not clearly understood. One of the reasons why it is difficult to explain how the suction is generated is the fact that the elephant has a fixed diaphragm, and suction is therefore not governed by independent movement of the lungs.

Elephants will readily wade into deep water to drink, but they usually drink from the bank of a river or pool. They have also been seen to wade into water and suck up the water directly into their mouths, but this is unusual. In keeping with their preference for clean drinking water they will often dig holes in sandy river beds a few metres from pools of water. They then drink the filtered water that seeps into the drinking holes.

THESE PAGES: WITH ELEPHANTS FEEDING IS AN ACTIVITY OF GREAT VARIETY ACHIEVED BY VERY DIFFERENT ACTIONS SUCH AS SIMPLY WALKING INTO A BUSH AND GRASPING BRANCHES WITH THE TRUNK (RIGHT); THE CO-ORDINATED ACTION OF THE TRUNK AND FEET IN DEMOLISHING A SHRUB (BELOW); OR CUTTING SHORT, NUTRITIOUS GRASS OFF AT GROUND LEVEL WITH A DEFT SWING OF A FOREFOOT (BOTTOM).

PAGES 70 & 71: AN ELEPHANT HERD IN THE SHALLOWS OF THE CHOBE RIVER, BOTSWANA DRINKING THEIR FILL (MAIN PICTURE). THE FLEXIBILITY OF THE TRUNK: STRETCHING TO SUCK UP LITRES OF WATER (BOTTOM LEFT) WHICH IS THEN POURED OR SQUIRTED DOWN THE THROAT (BOTTOM MIDDLE). IN DRY AREAS, ELEPHANTS OFTEN HAVE TO DIG IN THE SANDY RIVER BEDS IN SEARCH OF WATER (BOTTOM RIGHT).

These pages: Elephants employ a variety of techniques to gather food.

Pages 74 & 75: Young bulls practising the art of fighting. When adult, they often use these skills to deadly effect.

AFTERNOON

AGGRESSION, PROTECTION, DEFENSE

An elephant's tusks are among its most striking physical adaptations. Tusks are highly modified incisor teeth which, though also used for gathering and manipulating food, serve primarily as weapons. African elephants have few enemies, and it is a rare occasion indeed when an elephant calf is taken by lions. Adults are too large and powerful to fall prey to the big cats. But elephants evolved at a time when the dominant predator of the African savanna was a sabre tooth cat quite capable of killing an elephant. To defend themselves and their young against such monstrous predators, the elephants needed to be armed. Their tusks served this purpose admirably.

Elephants did not only need to defend themselves against predatory cats, however. In distant evolutionary times, as today, their most likely attackers were other elephants. Bulls have to fight for a position in the social hierarchy. This process begins when the animals are scarcely a year old, and continues until they are fully adult at the age of about 40 years. The bull's success in the fighting and sparring that determines his status relative to his companions depends upon his strength, his skill, and his tusks.

There are many preliminaries to a battle between elephant bulls. There is feinting and posturing, swinging of the head from side to side and rocking forward with head raised – partly to allow the bull to see his opponent clearly, but more likely to show off his tusks to best advantage, and so intimidate his adversary. Physical contact is initiated by a head-to-head clash. The bulls push against their opponent's head and tusks, grapple the opponent with the trunk and try to push with their full weight to force the adversary's head downwards. At the same time the fighting bulls also try to twist their opponent's head to one side to expose the throat and neck, which are the prime targets for a serious attack on another bull elephant. Usually a fight between bull elephants, especially young ones, is a ritualised affair and little or no damage is done. Only in serious fighting, as when one or both animals are in musth, is blood drawn. Then the victorious animal is quite capable of killing his adversary. The fatal wounds are usually in the neck and throat and there have been many cases of a tusk penetrating the skull and piercing the brain. There is little doubt from studies carried out in South Africa's Addo and Kruger parks that the main killers of adult elephant bulls are other elephants.

Among cows fighting is less serious. Disputes over waterholes, for example, are usually settled with ritualised displays and screaming at one another. There are many other behaviour patterns among cows, however, which are designed to protect their young against predators and which are quite clearly a behavioural form of defense. The intense social concern and contact shown towards babies by all herd members is just one of these mechanisms. When feeding the herd also tends to spread out with adult females and young bulls on the outskirts and the most vulnerable babies closer to their mothers in the centre of the herd. This usually means that the animals on the flanks are the first to detect predators such as lions or humans. They can then either see them off or warn the herd of danger.

The alarm behaviour of the "flankers" which consists of a roar, a trumpeting scream, a flapping of ears, or a dash towards the centre of the herd in the case of youngsters, elicits an instant response from the rest of the herd. The older cows immediately rush towards the source of the disturbance with heads held high, ears extended, and trunks up. The babies cluster behind and among the cows, where they are least vulnerable. There is also a rounding up behaviour in which all the youngsters move to the centre of the herd and the larger animals take up positions on the periphery. This ensures that no predator can get past the larger defenders and harm the young. This defensive behaviour was also adequate against primitive humans, but against modern man armed with high-powered rifles it is a death warrant.

In most cases where elephants come across lions, a quick charge at the predators is all that is necessary to send them running for cover. However, there are occasional records of lions feeding on young elephants. Perhaps the cats succeed in catching and killing them in some cases. There are also records of adult lions, working as a team, managing to kill elephants as old as ten years. The evidence of flattened vegetation around the sites of slaughter indicate that this was not easily achieved. It is also possible that in some cases the young elephants killed by lions were sick or injured. Such cases are most unusual, however.

People, and in particular visitors to national parks and game reserves in Africa, are usually intensely interested in the aggressive behaviour of African elephants. The behavioural patterns exhibited towards humans and predators are also used against vehicles in some places. In these areas it is not unusual for elephants to charge vehicles on sight. The fact that the vehicle rapidly moves off is interpreted by the elephant as a "successful charge". This reinforces the aggressive behaviour, which gradually spreads through the particular elephant population. This violent, aggressive behaviour was common in the Liwonde National Park of Malawi before tourism in vehicles became a regular occurrence. Once traffic levels increased and the elephants were regularly exposed to vehicles, their behaviour changed dramatically. They grew tolerant of vehicles and usually ignored their presence, or just moved away slowly from confrontations.

Elephants in national parks are relaxed in the presence of vehicles, but become agitated at the sight of people on foot. One must assume that their visual acuity is good enough for them to distinguish people inside vehicles, and there is also little doubt that they can differentiate the smell of humans from petrol, diesel and oil. Once the humans get out and are divorced visually from their vehicles, the elephants become alarmed and react by fleeing or by aggression. This behaviour is one of the reasons for a fundamental rule in African national parks – and that is that visitors must stay in their cars, unless escorted on foot by trained staff.

The efficiency of tusks as weapons is likely to be influenced far more by their sharpness and shape than their mere size. This may explain why young adult bulls spend more time rubbing their tusks against trees to "sharpen" them, than do cows or older bulls. The bulls that do the most fighting, i.e. animals that are in their prime and regularly experience musth from 25–40 years of age, have much sharper tusks than older or younger animals. The fact that cows keep their tusks relatively sharp also confirms the hypothesis that they should be seen primarily as weapons. For cows defend their young throughout life. Bulls, on the other hand, have less need of tusks as weapons once they have passed the age of 40 years, because they are then far less active in competing with other bulls for breeding. They also then make less effort to keep their tusks sharp and so there is less wear on them and they grow larger to develop into the enormous ivory of the great old bulls.

PAGES 78 & 79: A SKILLED FIGHTER TRIES TO PUSH HIS OPPONENT OFF BALANCE AND TO TWIST HIS HEAD AROUND TO EXPOSE THE VULNERABLE THROAT.

PAGES 80 & 81: AN ADULT BULL AT ETOSHA, NAMIBIA, SPLASHES IN A WATERHOLE WHILE A GEMSBOK CAUTIOUSLY WAITS HIS TURN.

PAGES 82 & 83: IN GENERAL ELEPHANTS ARE INTOLERANT OF THE CLOSE PRESENCE OF LIONS WHICH THEY WILL OFTEN HARASS OR CHASE AWAY (MAIN PICTURE), BUT DISINTERESTED IN OTHER UNGULATES (TOP AND BOTTOM RIGHT). PARASITES AND COMMENSAL INSECTS, SUCH AS THESE GREEN FLIES LAYING THEIR EGGS IN A WOUND, ARE PART OF AN ONGOING INTERACTION IN THE CYCLE OF LIFE.

BELOW: THE AGGRESSIVE BODY LANGUAGE OF AN ELEPHANT ABOUT TO CHARGE. FIGHTS USUALLY BEGIN WITH THE "HEAD HIGH" POSTURE WHILE ASSESSING AN INTRUDER. UNCERTAINTY MAY BE REFLECTED BY A TRUNK SWINGING FROM SIDE TO SIDE (RIGHT) OR BY LIFTING AND SWINGING A FOOT (FAR RIGHT). IN THE CHARGE THE TRUNK STARTS TO CURL UP (BOTTOM) UNTIL IT IS TIGHTLY CURLED UP UNDER THE CHIN WHEN THE ELEPHANT ATTACKS.

LEFT: WHEN CONSIDERING A CHARGE, AN ELEPHANT SEEMS TO BE STRAINING ITS SENSES OF HEARING, SMELL AND SIGHT TO ASSESS THE SITUATION.

ABOVE: A WEAKER BULL SHOWS HIS SUBMISSION BY ALLOWING THE DOMINANT BULL TO PRESS DOWN HIS HEAD.

BELOW & BOTTOM: WHEN UNCERTAIN ABOUT A CHARGE AN ELEPHANT MAY DEMONSTRATE ITS ANGER AND INTENTION BY DIGGING INTO THE GROUND WITH ITS TUSKS AND PRESSING ITS ROLLED UP TRUNK AGAINST THE GROUND. THESE ACTIONS ARE MOST COMMONLY USED TO KILL A MAN.

PAGES 90 & 91: SHATTERED WOODLAND IN THE LUANGWA VALLEY, ZAMBIA - MUTE TESTIMONY TO ELEPHANTS' ABILITY TO TOTALLY CHANGE THE HABITAT (INSERT). WHERE ELEPHANTS ARE LIVING IN REASONABLE BALANCE WITH THEIR ENVIRONMENT, BOTH VEGETATION AND ANIMALS THRIVE (MAIN PICTURE).

ELEPHANTS AND THEIR HABITATS

Only two species of animals in Africa are capable of transforming the environment. The prime modifier of the African landscape is our own species – modern man. The other is the African elephant. These two species can convert forest to woodland, and dense woodland with tall trees to open savanna or even grassland with a few scattered shrubs. And ultimately, when these large-scale vegetation changes are helped along by drought – a regular phenomenon in Africa – the degraded vegetation turns to unproductive scrub.

Where traditional African lifestyles are still practised, the modification of the habitat by man is principally by slash-and-burn agriculture. Cultivation requires that the land be cleared of its indigenous vegetation, especially trees, and replaced with food crops or cash crops. These are usually exotic plants that were brought to Africa over the centuries.

In the case of the African elephant the power to modify the environment rests in the animal's enormous body size, energy needs and behaviour. Adult elephants must consume 150–200 kg of plant material per day. This must be gathered efficiently, and for this purpose the trunk has evolved as a highly efficient organ to handle not only a great volume of food, but a great diversity. Elephants could never satisfy their food needs in arid regions if they were specialist feeders such as grazers, so their diet depends on variety. They select their food from grass, shrubs, herbs and trees, and dig it up from under the ground. Their feeding activities are therefore a great potential modifier of any African habitat.

It is not only the food requirements of elephants that govern their impact on the habitat, but also their sometimes wasteful and destructive feeding techniques. Elephants may break branches off trees, remove a few leaves and chew off some bark, and then discard the bulk of the material removed from the tree. They can uproot small bushes and saplings and even push huge trees over. These feeding actions can wreak devastation on entire thickets or patches of woodland. Furthermore, elephant bulls – who are the main culprits in the destruction of large trees – may be engaging in social activity, not feeding when they sometimes push trees over. It has been suggested that this behaviour in bulls may be a form of physical display to impress rivals with evidence of their strength.

The changes brought about by elephant feeding can be enhanced and accelerated by other factors, in particular drought and fire. When elephant feed on, and destroy trees and shrubs they open up forest and woodland. Conditions are then created where grass can grow with less competition for water and less shade from woody plants. The grass litter builds up and provides fuel for the annual dry season fires that sweep across the landscape. The more grass, the hotter the fire and the greater its capacity to do further damage to trees, and to destroy vulnerable seedlings. Fire then speeds up the process of opening up the habitat.

Elephants can also cause the death of trees by peeling off the bark, using their sharpened tusks as chisels. Once a small piece of bark is lifted from the wood, the elephant grabs it with its trunk and rips off long sections. The exposed wood is vulnerable to attack by insects such as wood borers, and also to fire, which damages the wood in the absence of the protective layer of bark. Sometimes elephants ring-bark a tree by systematically removing the bark all the way around the trunk, thus causing the death of the tree. There seem to be seasonal peaks in the debarking activities of elephants. This may be related to the onset of the new cycle of growth when the sap is rising after the dry season and the bark may be more nutritious.

The impact of elephant feeding and tree destruction is, however, not all negative. A growing body of evidence indicates that the African savanna ecosystem is well adapted to fluctuations in tree and elephant populations and that the activities of the African elephant have many positive ecological consequences for the habitat. The trees that are uprooted and fall over provide "tree top" browse at ground level for other herbivores such as impala, duiker and kudu. When elephants shake trees violently they produce a shower of fruit or pods often shared with other animals such as baboons, which are quite comfortable following a feeding elephant to snatch the odd fruit lying on the ground.

As felled trees die and decay, the minerals and nutrients locked up in the wood and roots are returned to the soil. Dead wood is also burnt and the ash fertilises the soil. Where the roots are ripped out of the ground leaves and litter accumulate, insects build homes, and an entire cycle of life is set into motion. Termites feed on the dead wood and are in time eaten by the specialist feeders like pangolins and aardvark.

Elephants have a major role, especially in forests, in spreading seeds and fruit through the environment. The seeds of many trees of the forest and savanna show enhanced germination rates after they have passed through the digestive tract of an elephant. The chemical action of the stomach fluids and the physical grinding action of the elephant's teeth presumably scarify the seed coat and allow for better penetration of moisture. There are even some forest trees whose seeds will not germinate unless they have passed through the digestive tract of an elephant.

For many animals, like francolin and other ground-dwelling birds, piles of elephant dung represent a useful collection of food items. Throughout Africa these birds can be seen busily scratching and pecking at the piles of droppings, selecting seeds and shoots from among the poorly digested material. Dung beetles and many other insects also feed on elephant dung. In one unique case the flightless dung beetle of Addo in South Africa is totally dependent on elephant dung for the food of its adults and larvae. The female beetle lays her egg inside a ball of elephant dung, which she buries under the soil. When the larva hatches it eats its way out of the ball, growing steadily as it does so. By the time it has eaten its way out, it is ready to pupate and change into its adult form as a beetle.

Whatever elephants do, their impact on the habitat is commensurate with their size, strength, and food demands. Elephants also have an impact upon a host of other animals and plants that share their environment. Many species of fungus pass through their entire life cycle in elephant dung. In some areas of the African savanna rivers only flow seasonally, and are reduced to sand-filled reservoirs for most of the dry season. Elephants can detect the water under the sand and are adept at digging holes into which the underground water trickles and filters. They drink their fill and move on – to be followed by many other animals which use the drinking holes created by the elephants.

PAGES 92 & 93: AN ELEPHANT HERD IN NAMIBIA.
IN A HABITAT WHERE THE DESTRUCTION OF TREES
WOULD BE SUICIDAL, ELEPHANTS SELDOM DAMAGE
THE VEGETATION (MAIN PICTURE). IN HIGH-RAINFALL
HABITATS WHERE THE VEGETATION RECOVERS
EASILY IT IS OF LITTLE CONSEQUENCE IF BUSHES OR
TREES ARE TOTALLY DEMOLISHED BY BROWSING
ELEPHANTS (INSERT).

THESE PAGES: A MAGNIFICENT TUSKER IN A
STRETCH OF MOPANE WOODLAND (KRUGER
NATIONAL PARK) THAT CLEARLY SHOWS SIGNS OF
ELEPHANT ACTIVITY (LEFT). REMOVING BARK IN
SMALL SECTIONS (TOP) DOES NOT HARM THE TREE.
THE RIDGED SOLE OF AN ELEPHANT'S FOOT IS HARD
ENOUGH TO WEAR PATHS IN THE SOIL SURFACE
(MIDDLE). A HEAP OF ELEPHANT DUNG ACTS AS A
NURSERY FOR MUSHROOMS (BOTTOM).

TOP LEFT: THE RED EARTH OF TSAVO, KENYA. THE COMBINED EFFECTS OF AN OVERPOPULATION OF ELEPHANTS AND DROUGHT HAVE REDUCED THE ONCE DENSE WOODLAND TO OPEN SCRUB AND BARE GROUND.

BOTTOM, FAR LEFT: IN TSAVO, LARGE ELEPHANT HERDS WITH VIRTUALLY NO CALVES WERE THE AFTERMATH OF THE MOST DRAMATIC ELEPHANT POPULATION CRASH IN MODERN TIMES.

ABOVE AND LEFT: WALLOWING ELEPHANTS CARRY AWAY SOIL AND MUD WHICH STICK TO THEIR BODIES. EVENTUALLY THIS CAN RESULT IN LARGE EXCAVATIONS AND THE TRANSPORT OF MUCH ORGANIC MATERIAL.

Above: An elephant bull demonstrates his enormous power by uprooting and carrying away an *Acacia nigrescens*.

Right: A solitary bull dwarfed by the grandeur of Damaraland.

Pages 100 & 101: Evening at Shingwedzi, Kruger National Park. The last rays of the setting sun silhouette an elephant against a cloud of dust.

EVENING

AGE AND DEATH

In a biological sense the death of an elephant, like the death of a person, is a perfectly normal event. But like people, elephants recognise that death has another meaning. While many other animals react to the deaths of their companions, it is usually no more than an instinctive and short-lived alarm reaction. But in the case of the African elephant other behaviour, not normally seen in other contexts, is brought into play in reacting to the death of one of their own kind. Elephants, like people, grieve.

Elephants have been seen to pick up the tusks, skulls and bones of dead elephants and carry them around, sometimes for long distances. They usually do not pass the carcass or skeleton of another elephant without paying some attention to it. This may involve picking up and smelling the bones or just gently wafting their trunk over the remains before slowly moving on.

Elephants will usually go to the aid of a sick or wounded member of the herd. There are many reports of bulls and cows propping up or supporting a wounded or injured comrade and showing great reluctance to leave an injured companion behind. This caring behaviour is commonly displayed by mothers towards their offspring, and by older female calves to youngsters. But it is also a behaviour of adults towards adults, and in this the elephant differs from other African animals. It is not surprising then that the reaction of elephants to their dead is also a complex and intensely social event.

In a typical elephant funeral observed in Addo in South Africa, the matriarch of a well-known herd had been killed by a bull in musth. The entire herd, including her young calf, was clustered around the body of the old cow. They greeted her by touching their trunks to her trunk and mouth, touched her all over, and tried to raise her. The calf was most insistent in greeting his dead mother, crying and screaming loudly. The rest of the elephants were initially quite vocal, but after a while they fell silent. The herd threw dust, soil and leaves onto the body, then tore up bushes and broke branches off trees, partly covering the body with them. For two days the herd kept up their vigil around the body. They wandered away from time to time to feed and visited a waterhole to drink, but spent most of the time standing around quietly near the body. Many other elephants from all over the park visited the body and tried to greet the dead matriarch. They sniffed and touched her, and often just stood around as though expressing quiet sympathy for the dead cow and her bereaved herd.

Another puzzling fact about elephants is that they don't only cover their own dead. There are many reliable records of elephant covering the bodies of hunters or other people that they have killed. Usually the bodies have been found under a layer of leaves, grass, branches and dust. The fact that elephants bury only elephants and humans is another strange link between the two species.

For wild animals in Africa death may have a wide variety of causes. Most are victims of predation – they are killed by any one of Africa's cats, torn apart by wild dogs, crunched by the powerful jaws of the spotted hyaena or dragged to a watery grave by a crocodile. Parasites and disease kill many animals, and starvation also takes its toll. For most African animals death in the jaws of a

carnivore is quick. The fate of the African elephant, however, is different. For elephants death, unless at the hands of man, is a slow process. Although there are a number of parasites and diseases that can kill elephants, their mortality is mostly linked to age. When an elephant's last set of molar teeth wears out and it can no longer feed properly, it slowly wastes away and dies.

In the case of cows, and especially the matriarch, the herd stays with her and helps to the end. Only rarely are old or sick cows left to die alone. For elderly bulls the comfort of the social life of the herd is only a dimly remembered experience. Most bulls spend their old age alone, or in the company of a few other bulls or "askaris". When the very old males lose condition and are close to death, the young bulls move on. When close to death the old bulls tend to stay near water, drinking when they can no longer eat. Eventually the animals are so weakened that they collapse, fail to muster the strength to rise, and then die.

The death of an elephant seldom goes unnoticed. Vultures see the carcass and fly in from great distances, gathering for a feast that will ensure the cycle of life continues. All the minerals and elements bound up in the elephant's body are released and passed on in the continual cycling of nutrients. But there is little that vultures can do to an elephant carcass other than peck out the eyes, the tongue and the soft skin around the anus. Even the sharp beaks of these carrion birds are unable to penetrate an elephant's thick skin. It is only when hyaenas or lions have opened the carcass, cutting through the skin of the belly, that vultures get their chance. Besides the flesh eaters, the body of an elephant provides a link in the life cycle of many other animals, such as blowflies. These insects lay their eggs on the body, and the larvae soon hatch and feed in the suppurating body juices of the carcass. The maggots feed and then dig their way into the soil, which is moistened by blood and shaded by the carcass. The maggots pupate underground and then emerge as adults to carry on the endless cycle of life in Africa.

Many other insects also feed on the carcass and then fly away to lay their eggs on leaves or in secluded spots. The damp ground where the blood and body fluids soak into the soil attracts flies and butterflies. The carcass also attracts dermestid beetles, small creatures that live on the skin, bones and hooves of various dead animals.

Once the carcass has been cut open and pulled apart by lions and hyaenas, the smaller scavengers like jackals have their turn. They take whatever titbits they can find. When the bones are exposed they are sometimes gnawed by porcupines. Every part of the elephant's carcass is fed upon by some creature or other, all playing the role of janitors of the wild. For most of the scavengers any old carcass will do. The lives of other specialised species, like the tinaeid moth, *Ceratophaga vastella*, are intricately linked to the elephant, however. This moth only lives where elephants are found, and it lays its eggs in the hardened soles of the dead elephant's feet. The foot soles, being harder than the rest of the skin, last much longer than the rest of the body. The soles separate from the rest of the skin of the foot and slowly curl up as they dry, forming a home for the moth. The larvae hatch and eat their way through the sole of the dead elephant. When they emerge on the underside they burrow into the soil, where they pupate. Eventually the adult moth emerges to continue its complex life cycle – which depends totally upon nourishment provided by the soles of the feet of a dead elephant!

The death of an elephant, therefore, means life to a host of creatures great and small. In life the elephant plays a vital role in the ecological continuity and functioning of the African ecosystem, and in death it serves a similar purpose.

PAGES 104 & 105: THE DEATH OF AN AFRICAN ELEPHANT - A BIOLOGICAL EVENT NO DIFFERENT FROM THE DEATH OF A MOUSE, BUT ON A VASTLY DIFFERENT SCALE.

PAGES 106 & 107: AN ELEPHANT BULL IN SAVUTI, BOTSWANA, PAYS HIS RESPECTS TO A DEAD COMPANION BY GREETING AND SMELLING AT HIM (MAIN PICTURE). THERE ARE MANY RECORDS OF ELEPHANTS PICKING UP AND CARRYING THE BONES AND TUSKS OF DEAD COMPANIONS (INSERT).

TOP LEFT & RIGHT: AN ELEPHANT CARCASS IS AN ABUNDANT FOOD SOURCE FOR A LION, SPOTTED HYAENAS AND NUMEROUS VULTURES, AND THEY WILL RETURN TO THE CARCASS DAILY UNTIL ONLY SKIN AND BONE ARE LEFT. PREDATORS MAY NOT SUCCEED IN OPENING THE TOUGH SKIN OF AN ELEPHANT CARCASS AND IT THEN DRIES ROCK HARD BEFORE ROTTING OVER TIME (ABOVE). THE BONES AND TUSKS OF MAFUNYANE, ONE OF THE MAGNIFICENT TUSKERS OF THE KRUGER NATIONAL PARK, WERE THE ONLY REMAINS A MONTH AFTER HIS DEATH (BELOW).

ABOVE: OLD ELEPHANTS, EMACIATED AND CLOSE TO DEATH, SPEND THEIR
LAST DAYS ALONE AND CLOSE TO A WATERHOLE.

RIGHT: IN SOUTHERN AFRICA A WASTING DISEASE OF THE TRUNK MUSCLES
MAY RESULT IN DEATH AS THE ELEPHANT CAN NO LONGER EAT OR DRINK.

PAGES 112 & 113: ELEPHANTS CONTINUE FEEDING THROUGH THE
NIGHT, THOUGH THEY MAY REST FOR A FEW HOURS.

PAGES 116 & 117: AN ELEPHANT SAFARI IN THE OKAVANGO SWAMPS IN
BOTSWANA IS AN UNFORGETTABLE EXPERIENCE.

PAGES 118 & 119: AT VITSHUMBE IN ZAIRE, PUPILS DO THEIR MORNING
EXERCISES WHILE AN ELEPHANT BULL STROLLS PAST - A RARE EXAMPLE OF
TOLERANCE AND MUTUAL RESPECT BETWEEN MAN AND ELEPHANT.

PAGES 120 & 121: THE RELENTLESS GROWTH OF HUMAN POPULATIONS
IN AFRICA, EVIDENCED BY THE VILLAGE OF KANYABAYONGO IN ZAIRE
(INSERT TOP LEFT) AND A GROUP OF MALAWIAN WOMEN, EACH WITH A
BABY ON HER BACK (INSERT BOTTOM LEFT) WILL, IN TIME, LEAVE LITTLE OR
NO SPACE FOR ELEPHANTS. A TRADITIONAL VILLAGE NEAR MANGO, TOGO:
CULTIVATION AND SETTLEMENT HAVE DESTROYED TREES AND TOTALLY
CHANGED THE ENVIRONMENT (MAIN PICTURE). ON THE EDGE OF A GAME
RESERVE AT FOSSE-AUX-LIONS, NORTHERN TOGO, THERE IS A MEASURE OF
CO-EXISTENCE BETWEEN DOMESTIC ANIMALS AND ELEPHANTS (INSERT TOP
RIGHT). AZAGNY, COTE D'IVOIRE (INSERT BOTTOM RIGHT): RAINFORESTS
ARE BEING DESTROYED SO RAPIDLY THAT ELEPHANTS WILL EVENTUALLY
SURVIVE ONLY IN NATIONAL PARKS.

ELEPHANTS AND MAN

Much has been written, here and elsewhere, about the relationship of modern man to the African elephant. This relationship has been dominated for the past two or three centuries by firearms – a product of the West. Yet the basic conflict and interaction between the two species goes back a very long time. The relationship has been based on respect as well as enmity, as indicated by 4 000-year-old rock engravings of elephants in the Sahara, the rock paintings of San artists and the petroglyphs of elephants at Twyfelfontein in Namibia.

While the competition between traditional African societies and elephants was predominantly for living space, it was never recognised as such by people. African society has no tradition of killing off elephants to be rid of them – that is a modern, post-colonial concept. Traditional African society respected the elephant but saw the need to protect crops and to hunt elephants for ivory and meat. To some extent the hunting of elephants was also seen as a challenge, as a test of manhood and skill the likes of which few modern peoples of the West could equal. To face and kill an elephant with traditional African weapons was an enormous, daunting task. It required true skill and courage, and the success of such an endeavour was always recognised. Elephant hunters were crowned with a dignity and esteem equalled only by that granted to lion-killers.

Elephant hunting is ingrained in the cultures of many African peoples. The technology and techniques differed according to the resources available and the conditions under which elephant hunting took place. Hunting an elephant in the depths of the rainforest, where elephants are secretive and occur singly or in small groups of two or three, is completely different from taking on the much larger herds found in the savanna.

The Khoikhoi, or Hottentots, who together with the Bushman or San people were the original inhabitants of South Africa, were renowned elephant hunters. Historical records indicate that their preferred technique was to use pit traps into which the elephants were driven. Once in the pits the elephants were despatched by spears or arrows.

The Pygmies of the rainforest were also elephant hunters. Their technique was to use a broad-bladed spear and to stalk an elephant in the forest. The hunter would try to approach the elephant unseen, preferably when it was resting or dozing. The spear would then be thrust up into the belly of the elephant. Death for the elephant was not instantaneous, but that was not particularly crucial. The Pygmies had the skill to track the wounded elephant through the forest, for days if necessary, until it died. Then the inhabitants of the hunters' village would be called to feast on the carcass. The skill required to approach an elephant up close in the forest can hardly be appreciated by a Westerner. For the Pygmy hunter detection meant death as it was difficult, if not impossible, to spear the charging elephant.

There are many records of the elephant hunting techniques of the Arabs of Sudan. These people had horses, which gave them an enormous advantage. The technique, however, called for a mounted swordsman to chase an elephant and get close enough to hack through the ligaments of the hind legs. Once this was done and the elephant immobilised it was speared, also with a broad-bladed

spear. An alternative technique called for the hunter to stalk the elephant on foot and slash its ligaments with a sword, before his mounted companions approached the animal to distract it from the man on foot.

The greatest elephant hunters of all time were undoubtedly the Wata people who lived in the nyika thicket country of Tsavo in eastern Kenya. The Wata used arrow poison and the most powerful handmade bows ever known. They hunted elephants using their traditional methods until the 1960s and so, fortunately, a great deal of information has been recorded about the methods and exploits of some of the greatest hunters of modern times. The Wata, also sometimes referred to as the Waliangulu, were hunter-gatherers who lived off the land. Their culture dictated that men should be hunters and they were taught this craft from boyhood. They lived in small groups or clans, were nomadic and could move to areas where chance rainfall provided a more bountiful harvest of food from the wilderness. Their skills extended not only to being able to kill elephants and black rhino efficiently, but also to reading all the signs of the natural world. They could read and interpret animal signs and tracks, understood animal behaviour to the finest detail, knew the uses of plants and had all the other knowledge needed to survive in a harsh and arid landscape.

The Wata made their powerful bows, with draw weights of 54 to 77 kilograms, from natural materials. Their arrows had razor-sharp iron heads, with flights made from vulture feathers. But the great secret of their skill was their knowledge and use of arrow poison. They extracted the poison from plants, and the most common one was a cardiac glycoside capable of paralysing heart muscles as great as those of an elephant. The Wata learned that the most vulnerable spot on an elephant was the lower left abdomen, where the arrow poison was absorbed fastest. They had the skill to stalk the elephants, select their quarry and shoot their arrow at its target. They ate elephant meat, but for centuries their objective was ivory, which they traded for everything else they needed from surrounding tribes. Sheep and goats, cloth, bracelets, and iron for arrowheads were all bartered for in ivory or rhino horn.

In many modern texts and magazine articles the Wata are described as cruel poachers who hunted inside the Tsavo National Park. The truth of the matter, however, was that the Wata were hunting elephants long before the birth of Christ. When the colonial authorities of Kenya proclaimed their traditional hunting grounds a national park in 1948, without consulting the Wata people, they were offered no alternative livelihood and carried on with their traditional lifestyle. They were then branded as criminals, harried and hunted, and their culture and society was destroyed. Yet they had played an important role in the ecology of the Tsavo area, and had probably even been the major factor in regulating the numbers of elephant in the area. When their offtake of elephants was stopped the elephant numbers increased, the habitat was destroyed and in a few years 20 000 elephants and 5 000 black rhino starved to death. People flooded into the park to collect ivory and rhino horn, then stayed to poach, and at the end of it all the Wata, the rhino and most of the elephants were gone.

Africans have never developed the same deep working relationship with elephants that Asians have. The only effort to domesticate elephants was undertaken by the Carthaginians. They used elephants for war, the most famous episode of which was Hannibal's march to Rome over the Alps in 218 BC. With the defeat of Carthage, the tradition of using elephants in North Africa died. It was briefly revived early in the 20th century in what was then the Belgian Congo when an elephant training centre was established near Garamba. Today only four trained elephants are left. More recently in South Africa and Botswana, trained African elephants have been used for elephant-back safaris, a unique and profitable way of using these animals. It is hoped that this enterprise will grow and become a more important chapter in the relationship between the African elephant and man.

PAGES 120 & 121: THE RAPID GROWTH OF HUMAN POPULATIONS, EVIDENCED BY THE VILLAGE OF KANYABAYONGO, ZAIRE *(INSERT TOP LEFT)* AND A GROUP OF MALAWIAN WOMEN, EACH WITH A BABY ON HER BACK *(INSERT BOTTOM LEFT)* WILL LEAVE LITTLE SPACE FOR ELEPHANTS. A VILLAGE NEAR MANGO, TOGO: CULTIVATION AND SETTLEMENT HAVE TOTALLY CHANGED THE ENVIRONMENT *(MAIN PICTURE)*. FOSSE-AUX-LIONS, NORTHERN TOGO: CO-EXISTENCE OF DOMESTIC ANIMALS AND ELEPHANTS *(INSERT TOP RIGHT)*. AZAGNY, COTE D'IVOIRE *(INSERT BOTTOM RIGHT)*: RAINFORESTS ARE RAPIDLY DESTROYED AND ELEPHANTS WILL EVENTUALLY SURVIVE ONLY IN NATIONAL PARKS.

LEFT: THE SAFARI HUNTING INDUSTRY PAYS A PREMIUM PRICE FOR BULLS LIKE THIS MAGNIFICENT TUSKER. MONEY GENERATED THUS CAN BE AN ABUNDANT SOURCE OF INCOME FOR TRIBAL COMMUNITIES IN AFRICA.

TOP: AUTHORITIES IN FOR EXAMPLE SENEGAL ARE FORCED TO SPEND SCARCE RESOURCES IN AN ATTEMPT TO CURB POACHING.

ABOVE LEFT: POACHERS USE A VARIETY OF WEAPONS.

ABOVE RIGHT: THE TUSKS OF MATURE ELEPHANT BULLS ARE STILL THE MOST SOUGHT-AFTER HUNTING TROPHY.

PAGES 124 & 125: THE ELEPHANT MANAGEMENT PROGRAMME IN THE KRUGER NATIONAL PARK INCLUDES THE IMMOBILISATION OF ANIMALS FROM A HELICOPTER TO FIT THEM WITH A RADIO TRANSMITTER COLLAR WHICH ALLOWS THE ANIMALS' MOVEMENTS TO BE MONITORED FOR UP TO THREE YEARS.

TOMORROW

ELEPHANT
MANAGEMENT

As the human population of Africa continues to increase, despite war and famine, so the range available for elephants and other wildlife will shrink. This is the lesson of African history as well as the developments of the post-colonial era. There are many examples which show that elephants are easily eliminated as a component of the African environment in the face of human population presence. Even in the relatively underpopulated Central African Republic, where there were as many as 60 000 elephants as recently as 1979, their numbers fell dramatically due to ivory poaching, to about 12 000 by 1991. While mankind can eliminate the African elephant, he can also restore the elephant to depleted ranges. This has been demonstrated in several countries where elephants had been greatly reduced in numbers at the turn of the century, but the species flourishes today.

In South Africa alone there were only 120 elephants in four scattered populations in 1920. As a result of sound wildlife management practices and effective protection, there are over 8 500 elephants today. However, the rehabilitation of the African elephant as a species requires expertise and technology. In Rwanda in 1973 the government decided to destroy the elephant populations of the Karama and Rwinzoka areas because of conflict with people. The adults were shot and 26 calves moved to the Akagera National Park. Today the population stands at 40 and it is increasing. A similar example is found in the Addo Elephant National Park of South Africa. In 1931 when the park was proclaimed there were 11 elephants; today there are nearly 200. Elephant conservation and successful management has been demonstrated – all that is now required is for us to decide where else we choose to repeat these successes, and how to sustain them.

There has been a traditional divergence in approaches to wildlife management in general, and elephant management in particular, between the southern African countries and countries elsewhere in Africa. In the south intervention was accepted from the start. When South Africa's Kruger National Park was proclaimed as a game reserve in 1898, for example, predator control was regarded as an essential management action. In East Africa the park authorities tried to run national parks without any active management other than controlling the traditional hunting of wildlife. A consequence of these divergent philosophies was that the national park authorities in South Africa were able to rescue several species of large mammals from the brink of extinction and build up their numbers to healthy levels. The managers of the Kenya national parks achieved the opposite and succeeded in bringing numbers of several once abundant species to the brink of extinction.

In South Africa the national park or game reserve is seen as an area isolated from its surroundings, which are inevitably populated and developed. Reserves have, therefore, been fenced to minimise contact and conflict across the boundaries. In the case of elephants the lesson of the incompatibility of the species with agriculture was learned early, and this led to the building of the world's first elephant-proof fence at Addo in 1953. This fence stopped all movement of elephants out of the park and eliminated the major source of mortality – shooting of crop-raiding elephants. The Addo range was, however, waterless and so the management of these elephants required the provision of pumped water right from the start. Fencing and provision of water became standard practice in any

wildlife management area. The other two major policies of interference are the controlled use of fire to achieve a desired physiognomy or structure of vegetation, and the control of animal numbers.

In time it was realised that a basic scientific understanding of the dynamic nature of the functioning of ecosystems was essential for management. The dynamics of fire ecology, the relations between predators and prey, and the impact of herbivore species on grasslands and savannas had to be understood. This led to the development of research sections in the major wildlife management agencies, and a strong scientific underpinning of elephant management in particular.

The monitoring of elephant populations requires regular counts. These can be either total aerial counts as done in some parks, or sample counts from which extrapolations are made to larger areas. Counting of elephants provides data on whether populations are increasing or decreasing. More refined data, however, are derived from assessments of the population composition and in particular from the size of the annual calf crop. Techniques have been developed whereby the age structure of elephant herds can be derived from measurements taken from aerial photographs of the animals. Because elephants can have such a profound impact on the vegetation of national parks it has become necessary in areas where intense elephant management is practised to monitor the status and trend of plant communities and in particular to track those changes brought about by elephants such as the destruction of woodland.

Elephant movements have also been intensively studied to enable us to understand their social behaviour, to assess their impact on the habitat, and more recently to study the disturbance effect of culling operations on elephant clans or kinship groups. These studies were made possible by advances during the 1960s in the technology of the chemical immobilisation of animals. The development of drugs such as M99 and its antagonists made it possible to immobilise adult elephants for marking operations and then to revive them as a matter of routine. Originally elephants were darted, marked with painted numbers and ear streamers and revived. These animals were then followed for as long as the paint lasted – which turned out to be three weeks or so at the most. The next step was to fit the elephants with colour-coded and notched collars made of machine belting. Then, after further technological progress, the fitting of miniaturised radio transmitters to the collars became standard practice. Individual elephants could then be tracked from the ground or the air for periods as long as three years. The ultimate development has been to fit elephants with transmitters that can be located automatically by satellite and so give an hourly fix of the elephant's position 24 hours a day.

In addition to these advances there have been many dedicated scientists working on the behaviour and ecology of elephants. Their work has accumulated into an enormous body of information which makes the elephant one of the best-known African mammals today. In addition studies on the reproductive physiology, feeding, nutrition, growth, water requirements, genetics and many other aspects of elephant biology and ecology have been carried out and provide a sound basis for elephant management.

In southern Africa, where increasing elephant populations have put pressure on the vegetation of national parks, culling has been carried out as an essential tool in managing elephant population density. Products resulting from culling operations are meat, skins and ivory. The revenue derived from the sale of these products has been ploughed back into elephant management and protection. This is particularly relevant as it has been shown that in the face of poaching a well-paid and efficient guard force is necessary to ensure the survival of elephant populations.

ELEPHANTS KILLED IN A CULLING PROGRAMME AIMED AT MAINTAINING A BALANCE BETWEEN THE ANIMALS AND THEIR HABITAT. CULLING IS THE ONLY SOLUTION IN NATIONAL PARKS WITH A LIMITED CAPACITY TO SUPPORT GROWING ELEPHANT POPULATIONS.

One of the most positive aspects of culling operations in South Africa and Zimbabwe has been the rescue of calves. During these operations family groups are killed, but calves between about one and five years of age are captured and translocated to establish new elephant populations in areas where the species had been extinct, in some cases for 150 years. More than 30 such populations have been established since 1979, and in at least two of these translocated calves have grown up, despite the trauma of capture and translocation, and successfully bred. This indicates beyond doubt that elephants can be conserved anywhere in Africa, for the future.

PAGES 130 & 131: CULLING IN THE KRUGER NATIONAL PARK IS UNDERPINNED BY A RESEARCH AND MONITORING PROGRAMME. AN ADULT COW FITTED WITH A RADIO TRANSMITTER IS STIMULATED BY A RESEARCH ASSISTANT (MAIN PICTURE). THE RADIO SIGNALS FROM THE COLLAR CAN BE MONITORED FROM THE GROUND (INSERT LEFT) OR FROM THE AIR. AN IMMOBILISED ELEPHANT IS CAREFULLY MEASURED BEFORE THE RADIO COLLAR IS FITTED (MIDDLE INSERT). A MINUTE AFTER THE ANTIDOTE TO THE IMMOBILISING DRUG HAS BEEN INJECTED (INSERT RIGHT) THE ELEPHANT REGAINS FULL CONCIOUSNESS AND GETS UP.

PAGES 132 & 133: CULLED ELEPHANTS ARE THOROUGHLY BLED IN THE FIELD TO ENSURE USABLE MEAT (MAIN PICTURE). CULLING IN HWANGE NATIONAL PARK, ZIMBABWE: ANIMALS ARE NUMBERED AND THEIR SKINS REMOVED IN PANELS TO PRODUCE FINE LEATHER (TOP INSERT). IVORY WAS THE MOST VALUABLE BY-PRODUCT OF CULLING BEFORE THE CITES BAN ON THE IVORY TRADE (MIDDLE INSERT). ELEPHANT MEAT FROM A ZIMBABWE CULL IS DRIED BEFORE BEING SOLD TO THE LOCAL POPULATION, THUS SERVING AS AN IMPORTANT SOURCE OF PROTEIN (BOTTOM INSERT).

THESE PAGES: VISITORS TO NATIONAL PARKS ARE KEEN TO VIEW WILDLIFE AT CLOSE QUARTERS (MAIN PICTURE). PARKS ARE REQUIRED TO SPEND LARGE SUMS ON SECURITY AS ILLUSTRATED BY THESE RANGERS ON PATROL IN THE TEMBE ELEPHANT PARK, KWAZULU (LEFT), AND THE ELEPHANT-PROOF FENCE IN ADDO (RIGHT). CULLING IN THE KRUGER NATIONAL PARK HAS YIELDED HUNDREDS OF YOUNG ELEPHANTS THAT CAN BE TRANSLOCATED TO ESTABLISH NEW ELEPHANT POPULATIONS THROUGHOUT AFRICA (FAR RIGHT).